MOODS

Rachel B. Glaser

Published by Factory Hollow Press
a Division of Flying Object

Flying Object Center
for Independent Publishing,
Art, & the Book, Inc.
Flying Object is a 501(c)(3) nonprofit
art and publishing organization.

Factory Hollow Press c/o Flying Object
42 West Street, Hadley, MA 01035

www.flying-object.org
www.factoryhollowpress.com

Cover Design by Rachel B. Glaser
Interior Design by Pam Glaven, Impress, Northampton, MA
Front Cover Image by Rachel B. Glaser
Back Cover Image by Sam Pulitzer
Printed by The Studley Press, Dalton, MA

ISBN 978-0-9795905-4-2
Copyright © 2013 by Rachel B. Glaser

The poems in MOODS first appeared (often in a different form) in "Heroes Are
So Long" (a *Minutes Books* chapbook) and the following journals: *Notnostrums,
Invisible Ear, GlitterPony, Noo Journal, Everyday Genius, Jubilat, Supermachine,
Two Serious Ladies, Skein, Sprung Formal, Wolf in a Field, New Delta Review,
Death Hums, 3AM, Wigleaf, MLP Stamp Stories, Dewclaw* and Jupiter 88.

For JT

CONTENTS

Sleeping ugly moon

my soul was swimming
and ruined all my good clothing

I was damp and God offered me a drink
his voice descended
"Well done woman, let me gaze your naked heart"

God's mighty arm jumped carelessly roof to roof
disturbing peaceful sleeping
I was reluctant and he said
"I will give you a golden ray"

I drew my shirt close
for I already had a golden ray

it was old, but still worked
I used it on the stairs at night
and occasionally during the day

God scratched and clouds scattered
a big wave came and broke my shirt

God's vision handled my bosoms
"I've handled hundreds and hundreds of bosoms"
said God
his eyes shone with weeping

Playing ping-pong on the Wii, it's hard not to channel the McEnroe/Borg HBO documentary

and when cooking with olive oil I feel this pretty strong
European-decadence feeling I'm not sure where I learned
it is a boring life, but each text from an ex
feels like the Uprising

spiders spindle out the ancient past
lovers fall into a liquid dream

even in a dull life, bits cling to a better idea
my neck hurts and I wonder about the pain
it's an *Egyptian* pain! I decide at once
pleased as if I just personalized a web-pet

in our hot, moldy hall we are prisoners
but my hair dries right and I am royalty

yesterday we were invited out
and became naturally young and worldly
laughing made us stretchy
when it thundered we felt cozy and provincial

today, inside like a bug and silent for hours
I feel like a genius with social problems
we put on Woody Allen and
there is a new oldness to the room

my hair frizzes, and I think
oh, that's so typical of me
but I don't understand what I'm saying
I'm tired and there is an Old Testament quality to it
because sleep is religious
I've known this and forgotten
and remembering is female

there are the women of the past
(brushing the hairs of a wild fire)
and the women of the future
(coolly zapping a dlonze)
and these women are all represented as a graphic of lines
in the terrific logo on a shampoo bottle

but there are times this slow life has no thoughts
the associations shrivel
the towels look truly pathetic
my neck hurts
and in no interesting way

Donna and her sister

Donna and her sister were ruining his life
"Hi Sal!"
"Hey," Sal said quietly
he left them alone at the plant store

Sal was 29
when he felt tired, he took himself back to his apartment
"Love!" Donna's sister cried as Sal took off in his car

the whole town was Donnas and sisters
in the library one said, "I'll control you"

they were in the Whole Foods parking lot
when he felt himself grow calm
it rained lightly and Sal thought they were crying

they made pancakes and ate them but Sal couldn't taste
them
"You switched from human to boring," Donna said
her sister nodded robotically

Sal felt frozen
the sex had been diagnostic
"I'm not what you need, I think," Sal said slowly
to help them

Heroes are so long

any fault of theirs is good

a one wrapped in fives
a surgery for fun

the passed down stay up
a nose
dishes
other things lay down

one time I lost a mortal god a dog soul the fate smell
I knew all haunting was privilege
that a wish can be 3-D

there'd been grace around
and it fell all over

a dick is a thick way to say it
a telephone is a place to reform it

a mother reiterates
we recite
recite
sing

believe ghosts
suppose all kinds of mirrors

heroes are gilded then golden so long
they didn't do anything wrong

I like what they did wrong

Smith social experiment

these girls, some of them are writing poetry
in their head full-time
in the sun and the shade

having just eaten lunch
in a blissful between–class state
some are wrestling in the grass

an armless girl moseys on by
here is a safe place for an armless girl, her parents said
to one another

these Smith girls are filled with atoms
being around each other is like
bananas being around bananas
they are almost never not getting their periods

Thanksgiving didn't happen

let's breed your family dog with my family dog
your religious beliefs with mine
we can say Jesus existed
he was good looking, charismatic
and once did a magic trick

if we still hate the cat tomorrow
let's tie him to the tracks

when we all smoked catnip together, I lied
I did feel different

something else I didn't tell you was
when I was in the WNBA
I had a very poor shooting streak and couldn't admit it
I'd miss a three-point attempt
and pretend it was an ally-oop
"Where were you Swoops?! The ball was there," I'd say,
"But where the hell were you?"

I'm not joking, I'm crying
Julia Roberts won a Golden Globe
and I'm about to get my period
maybe I'll get it now
or now

when I touched your nose before, it was a signal to God
this one, please put this nose on my kid
when I have one, this nose
when I have one, this kid

all I know is one thing:
hairs really love to grow out of a mole
a homerun feels nice cuz everyone can take their time
people marry easy and it's like playing Blackjack scared

also, that Thanksgiving didn't happen how they said
all it was, was two Indian boys
who shared some deer meat with two Pilgrim girls
and (big surprise)
their families freaked out
the girls got sent to boarding school
the boys were sent into the woods to "think"

and not even the same woods
the boys were sent to two different woods
that were very far apart
one of them died

Every time my pills fall, I feel very much like an addict

when they scatter, it is disapproving
they dance on hardwood
they rest on carpet

it is maddening to spill pills across a restaurant floor
children clap
women are exhilarated
I want to lie on my rug and self-reflect
but my hair goes limp
I am late for the train

spilling pills makes me feel like I have a stressful, high-profile job
that I really have no time to pick up anything
I have too many young kids
the landline is crammed between my cheek and shoulder
like a sex addict
like I have a shoplifting problem
or I've borrowed people's kids
despised people's pets
impulsively pulled the fire alarm
I have denounced my enemies on television
I have seduced my daughter's boyfriend
I have read my husband's diary

I want to be calm
I wish I could appreciate humor/nature

I feel like an addict when I arrive late to a dinner party
when I eat at Brueger's during certain times of day
when I find myself drawn to big jewelry, and basements

and one of the pills is at least three years old
it crumbles in the breeze
it is held together barely

it is a Valium
it probably doesn't work

I feel like a hoarder when I see the Valium
like somehow somewhere I have held onto all my hair

also, I think it's sort of corporate when a cell phone
rings in public
I feel hapless eating pizza

like I'm drunk if I park weird

whenever I see someone with a prescription pill bottle
I assume they are insane

they are fried
very dangerous

if I see someone yelling at a bus driver
or in a park by themselves

if I see someone walking anywhere near a highway
or if someone closes their eyes on a subway

I see an elderly lady with a sunburn
or a grown animal crying

I look away and then I look longer

if I see someone take a pill in public
I am visibly uncomfortable
if I am in the elevator with one person
forget it

I feel rebellious when rejecting my cable company
I ignore policemen and eat at the salad bar
I drop electronics in water

a child in a store is hostile to me

I always thought if I shaved my head I would suddenly

become adventurous
and have more friends
I'd be able to sculpt or at least be musical

I wouldn't be afraid
I would look younger and more troubled
I'd crash at someone's house or they would crash here
my hair would inch out and I'd have a choice

I think if I grew it very long, I'd make money
I would have to go swimming all the time

it would be like a fur and babies would grab it
I would laugh and leaves would rustle
and this would all be in the sunshine

unless it was a failing ponytail
like I had been too stubborn in my style
and it had crusted over

but really the ponytail is a good one
it is rural
and aural
people see me and think I cook well
if I don't have children, someone encourages me to
out of curiosity

I smile and take a pill
if I have a runny nose
or aches and pains
if I don't have to drive anywhere
if it's a weekend
and no one is free
I go for the Valium
but it laughs itself into dust
like it's exhausted
like it's gone extinct
like it's anti-drugs

Two girls can talk about two boys and make it sound like a conversation

the girls are on beds or porches
they are using their reasoning
to walk themselves like dogs to the store
they are terrified to have children and
get lost in the vast, unimaginable plane

abstract and promiscuous friends drop by during long,
boring nights of drinking
the town is so bare, that when one person says
something memorable another person has the time
to write it down

the summer makes them immortal
all the memories arrive in a bundle from last summer

the boys are immediate
one is crouching over, his butt visible to house guests
they are comparing books
they are sampling the local beer
they are carving their personalities into the wood
they are making the night ridiculous

the day becomes an orphan madhouse
alone with either of the boys

in social situations, the girls are still
watching the interlocking planes
this is a town where there is room
the money rests
a boy lets his habits become little, meaningless myths

Best nose

"Lucky me," Mom said, "best nose!"
Janey wanted surgery so we all crowded
around the mirror
Mom gave us old photographs to look at
"Phillis was lucky," Mom said, "best eyes!"

Phillis is our lost sister who ran off when she was young
she used to laugh when we were naked and in a circle
of four, pressing our breasts to our sisters' breasts

she used to let the dog lick her mouth
while we all played cards in the kitchen

we began to cry, Phillis was very unlucky in fact
she had left home and when she tried to return
mother pretended not to recognize her
though she had grown very beautiful
we cried from the upstairs window
she returned to California
without stepping foot in our house

the more we cried, the uglier we got, according to mother

"Who has the best hair?" I asked, though I knew the answer
Hattie blushed and mother laughed

"Your hair wouldn't be any good if I didn't wheel it in
curlers!"

it was true
each week we watched in boredom as mother rolled
Hattie's hair

the phone rung
"It's Phillis!" we shrieked
as we always shriek when the telly rings

I tore across the room to answer it

"Hellooo," Phillis said
in the sly way they talk in Hollywood
"Heloooo!" we said in unison, crowded around the receiver

Should I learn another language?

No! I'm getting married on a boat in five minutes
I'm having a baby on the table
I'm elaborately renewing my vows
my child is screaming
my husband is aging
our house is built at a slant
our neighbor is punting our cat
our son is so flaky
my daughter is dating
my dog's now a grandpa
my career is soaring!
my daughter is bankrupt!
my ailments are combining

Can I take a minute to call my dear friend from college?
How we walked together, to and from school. Her ideas
were revolutionary. Her husband is hilarious. She has
billowy, black hair.

my curls are confusing!
my husband is suing
his eyes are like fish eggs
his hair is arresting
the clouds are so skinny
the weather's redundant
our president is pretty

my eyelids are crusty
my husband's in rehab
my children run prisons
my legs sound like attics

I go back to college. I'm old but I'm working. My
dorm makes me silly. My body goes backwards.

my teeth get too whitened
I'm back a few birthdays
I'm young and I'm scheming
my boyfriend's proposing
I wish I was older
my math test sucks big time
my best friend smokes Winstons
my allowance is puny
my pet is the best thing
I live with my parents
I'm kind but I'm daring

Camp

at camp everyone was hot but we never touched
the names in the wood were romantic to us
we imagined saying Owen into the night
(how mournful and wonderful)
Leo!
(the O yelling out to the moon)
at camp, and only in love with ourselves!
The outdoors!
(and ourselves!)
Owen!

I took a secret trip to have an affair

but wanted to call my wife the whole time
I wondered what shows she was watching

I knew since I was gone
my wife was living in a forbidden, wanton way
I knew for instance, that she was leaving things
where she had used them
not where they belonged

if she had cooked, the dishes still sat around like guests
the dog was in the bed

I slept with my lover and it was a strenuous ordeal
I could see my wife eating popcorn through it
waiting it out

afterwards there was no leisure
as travel is just stress over leisure

there was leisure but it was foreign

my arms brushed against my lover
all the things I didn't know about her lived inside her
like barnyard animals

my wife was beyond it all
splayed out on our old couch
in the middle of a long stare at the ceiling fan
made hallucinatory by light and a lack of responsibilities

when I excused myself to the bathroom
my lover hesitated in bed
and her mood sunk to unknown depths
she could tell I held my phone
like a key away from the world

Feminine in water

a way to keep hair good is to use goo
she tries this and feels sexy

she struts around her condo
does her nails and feels fancy

she sings and feels worthwhile
cries and feels fertile
then she calms down

she is lucky
she realizes
many women only feel feminine in the water

near dolphins
or when a saxophone sweats and strains

many feel feminine when a black man is in the room
when an egg wiggles ass in a pan
when a cop interrupts her evening

a motorbike rumbles beneath her
a refrigerator turns its light on

a dog is enthusiastic
or her meal is very delicious

other women only feel feminine in the air
piloting planes
jumping rope

water stays close to a woman in pools
pasta swirls on her fork

a woman laughs uproariously while digging a trench
daintily arranges the knick-knacks on a detective's desk
sits in trees with birds in her hair
she ignores what I've said
running her finger down a dusty antique mirror

what is feminine?
a towel baked in the sun
a monument with carved hair
a wild animal's cursive handwriting

My common lover

if my lover isn't a prince of a nation
he is at least a dangerous man with style

Augustine wore a zebra carcass
his hair wound around a hunk of jewel

Herman dressed smartly
and gifted me a diamond fork

I am a noblewoman
small inside a castle of cold stones
covered in furs and woods and drapes

a coat closet
a dress closet
sentimental rugs reflecting in many eyes of crystal

the only common lover I ever took
was a man with a golden voice
that made women unconsciously lean forward

when he said my name aloud
I felt enormous pride for myself

to greet this man I had a new wardrobe made

one that used expensive and rare fabric
but in a less ornate fashion

the eyes of the common lover grew glassy
when he stepped foot in my castle
so I redid one of the wings in a more understated style

nights we lay in bed and he told me of his modest life
no, I told him gently, tell me again of mine

God is popular

god is popular with athletes
they think about him while they practice
but rarely will he watch with one of his eyes

he has countless eyes
a hundred eyes, more
he is all eyes, but they hurt
and he can never sleep

the ocean is okay
but boats crowd it with their wakes
god can't help but look at every bubble

it puts a strain on his eyes to watch small things
and fast things
cities, streets, fingernails
dots on a die

he prefers to watch other planets
Saturn and those ones
those are graceful
more one color

watching Rushmore be built
the Great Wall
something lengthy and accumulative

he hates fireworks
but the worst is to see a needle being strung
the little end of the string struggling to fit
his eye feels like it's been injected with iodine

he cannot rub it
he is invisible
no one can help him

My electric guitar got soft over time

apocalypse means everyone dies and we are left
like when the football game stopped so we could 69
then the game resumed and your team had lost

football is cocky badasses in costume
basketball is the soul game of the body

I can get cozy understanding this moment
but then I'm unprepared for the next

you screwed my girlfriend
all my loose-leaf paper
my parents flipped out
my dog was disappointed

my rabbi bewitched a teenager
the teenager was hospitalized
the hospital was graffitied

my graffiti was scrubbed by city workers
my graffiti you can still see to this day

my girlfriend did you
and she does it really good

I'd be a badass if I didn't feel so bad about my body
my family wasn't dysfunctional
I was the only one
my guitar was blue and then it bled

Sing radiohead like something has gone wrong

karaoke is praying
if you do it right
biblical holograms of high school bedrooms
your voice reflecting in the glass

in a bar in a town where we had re-found each other
they wheeled out the old songs
from when we were young with other people
a little t.v. with words

a person would go up
sing good or sing weird

Drew knew a way to sing a song about the song
from within the song
everyone laughed and dated their friends

and what about the music we made in cars
when no one was sitting shotgun
no one carrying the radio like a football (snug) (well)

no poetry looked so humble as the kind flowing
up the screen
the color moving left to right
each word getting wet

Drew found the center and squeezed
he destroyed songs until they were just embarrassing
stories about yourself

Incest is lazy

a graveyard's relaxing
the police are pretentious
artists are wimps
jocks are blocks
babysitters are prostitutes
angels are gay
holidays are non spontaneous
moms are my slaves
dads are hard to read
homework is lame
Sundays I find mournful
gossip is energy
love is overdone
birds don't participate
brothers are renditions
teenagers are accused
beer is filling the room
globes are spinning off their holders
boogers are extra atoms
science is sexy
history is impossible
Kathy is unholy
Sarah is hella lonely
butts are like babies
writing is like boring
boys eat power

baseball season is over
fall is like grunge music
days are alike
hell is not real
heaven is fake
balloons are so obvious
triangles have a sly vibe
newspapers bore children
man oh man
ping pong is a happy sport
candles give a room motion
frozen meals lack a life
friends are brief masterpieces
weed is so crazy
America was immoral
humans are monsters of choice

Grand Variety

at the Community College where I clean
the students are virgins of stone
and I stick my blue gum into the carved wrinkles
in their jeans

the girls show their lust in run-on sentences
while a tiny mustache grows on a young jock/slacker

I am an actress so
whatever job I take on is a performance
especially when I mop the gym floor

far from the small campus
in the stark light of my cramped apartment
my date has a CVS brand orgasm
and I buy a Nike one on my smartphone

I'm not that athletic but I like how it feels

my parents have a lot of Price Club orgasms
but I will never be like them

an orgasm at the Community College might tickle
the face of a nun
and freeze the students into a coma/sculpture state

but still, once in a while
I have a knock off Versace orgasm quietly in the trees

an orgasm pushes you far away from yourself
rushing you to the end of your life
almost every company has one

in the west coast there are a lot of start-up orgasms
very difficult to classify
and an ergonomic one I have bookmarked the tab to

some girls can only have JCrew orgasms
those are good too (in the Fall)

during a sun shower I dust the Community College
the students forget their homework
and their virginity is forced upon them again
like Disney VHS tapes and Old Spice deodorant

in the waiting room at an audition for a cartoon voiceover
I find myself pretending to be a College student
I fold my legs underneath me, check my phone, and sigh

exhausted in my bedroom (which is covered in wall
hangings the last tenant left behind)

I fool myself into a nap, but a PayPal rep wakes me
I want us to have an Excel orgasm together
a Tupperware one, or Nature's Pride
but I barely know her

while everyone is partying and succeeding in nyc
and all the cities in my computer's time zone list
I turn on all the lamps to raise my confidence
the wall hangings look on with folky, unfinished faces
how haggard I feel having a Land's End orgasm
though my breasts don't know the difference

Staring into the Eyes of an Animal

an animal is not moral
and it's relieving

an animal stares the way a tree regards a stranger
it sees but doesn't find seeing so exciting

an animal makes no parade of its day
it takes the sun
takes the heat

flies fly noisy and random
birds peck as if particular

cows are not careful or concise
but watch them stare a hole into something

the way they mate
their stoicism
their texture
it is difficult not to hold an animal in too high esteem

staring into the eyes of an animal
the animal will not unwind
the starer is met with the animal's godly nonchalance
the animal's stupid intelligence
the animal's blah attitude on things

staring into animal eyes is an earthly tradition
when a soldier feels solemn
or a teenager angsty
a lady feels demolished
and a man feels disheveled
they go outside for an animal
find the eyes and look into them
because animals alleviate human pain

the eyes make them shudder
the soldier is scheduled
the teenager, unpopular
the lady is done for
the man is uncleanly

animal eyes are roaming judges
they are historic and unsentimental

me and you wait for Our Husband
though he's only so-so

your roommate thinks I'm sexy
my roommate thinks you're sexy

we wake up sexy from this
but it fades

Our Husband is coming, you tell me at the party
he is someone you like, but dreamed that I married
the party is nothing
it is before Our Husband

during the rainstorm we passionately text x boyfriends

my x boyfriend freezes his sperm in an ice cube tray
your x boyfriend does xtreme stunts in the snow

Our Husband arrives to little applause
his handsomeness is wasted
he bikes uselessly towards us in the rain

I'm dead

i'm dead, she said, I'm just
still hanging around

her body was hollow
but the right shape

everyone gets where they're going
the cue ball sends solids to sleep-away camp
a hug puts people in a temporary place

this was the overtime
her wig looked fine
not at all flat

she said not to eyeliner on
too many eyebrows
and I always listen at advice

a boyfriend shouldn't smash your records down the stairs
a cheerless living situation turns a year towards itself

I'm not without convictions
Hollywood should cut more film to the floor
religion is a club and
you don't have to root for the home team

someone fainted
taking attention away from her

we all hung around resembling each other
redid her nails since the people had taken it off
didn't know if she'd die again or something worse

the body inevitably misbehaves
but that's how we bought it

time spills
an eight-ball gives plot

I'm dead, she said
and made a face

we stayed up late and families usually don't

The BAD LOFT PARTIES

I had sex with this boy I'm friends with. He has such
a nice girlfriend. If the parties hadn't been so bad, we
wouldn't of, but every party was bad. One party had
baked ziti, but was still bad. The friend, he wears
t-shirts that have disgusting things silk-screened on. Like
somebody eating their eyeball with a fork. Somebody who
is not real. Or a cow having sex with a car and both are
dripping with slime. A bathtub filled with blood but the
blood has a smile.

My friend decided to write a love song to win back his
girlfriend. I helped because I took Poetry once, so I know
how to do lyrics. We tried to make a song but it sounded
too somber. I think it's because both our guitars are black,
I said. He looked and it was true. Shit, these are my only
guitars, he said. But it was O.K. A love song is always sad.

I have never made anyone my whole world. I like tak-
ing apart bikes and putting them back together different.
There was never a guy who floored me. The ones I know,
you'd be retarded to get lost in. They live in basements
and pee in bottles. They steal everyone's Netflix. A party
that's bad, makes me more sad than mad. That's one of
my lines from my poems. Then it goes: A boy is a body, a
butt is so bare, I ride on my bike, no hands, eating air.

Your soul, barely

your soul was hidden with hair
had on it, a few proud moles the witchdoctor believed
to be normal

we were outside on a towel
my soul was lit up and obvious
yours was obscured, unusual and unwilling

you were the pet falcon of an old woman
you were a child's best trousers
do you like the drums?
you were a drunken songbird put in with owls
do you smell the odor of a garden?
did you tell your mother you felt ill?
you got tired of talking and left the tavern

an arrow, you sped from the bow
and pierced the eyes of villagers

it was morning
the children cried

you called it an illusion
you called this world a phantom world
you were still sharp
no one could hug you without bleeding

you were friends with angels
and the angels got injured

you were not concerned
your eyes were hot
you would not relax
the Blinded cursed you
and the sound of your name
moved your body like a song

you stabbed eyes and crops
and the bedding of your neighbors

you fell on the rooftop and leaked
you were dead, but glumly went and got ready to die
the man at the cemetery pointed the way
but you didn't go

you couldn't give up wanting to be famous
you worried about what you were going to eat
you wanted to buy an engraved belt

we grew tired of you
so you turned into a rare bird to awe us

the townspeople watched you freak out in the fountain

you were trying to make money
you pranced and looked sick
you were wearing an engraved belt

Lon and his family

Lon shot a burglar in the fall. Life gave him no more
joy. His family worried. He was immune to fun. It
didn't catch him. It happened around him. His young
granddaughter threw her doll at his crotch and every-
one laughed, but Lon picked up the wooden woman and
gave her back to Philene. His wife breathed the easy
sleep of the normal. Lon felt the indifference of blind
objects. His house, which they'd put together with such
intuition and infatuation, was like a joke cemented in place.

The burglar was tall and fell to his knees and twisted.

Philene had her choice of many toys, but only Floreece
slept in the bed. Floreece had a jaunty mouth. Her
wood often splintered. Philene knew she could learn
from Floreece. Floreece was older.

Buying money

I really miss buying money
I would use my socks and my candy
a good alternative for someone with old items

the pink toaster
feather headdress
cute lamp
Merlin's hat
solar calculator
troll in raincoat
barbie's bad shoes
trick ice cream cone
frisbee with local advertising
Amy Grant cd
medieval lego man
Club Med trophy
homemade doll parachute
dinosaur-shaped notebook
deluxe toothbrush set
pet balloon

I would lay it out on the trundle

this was usually after we ran the pro races
he wore the entire pro athletic clothing set

(shoes, vest and shorts)
my pocket was puffed with cash

we ran one pro race per day
then bathed
and did homework

I knew about money
that it piled exact and thin
it bundled in families and waited in suitcases
it could turn at any moment into a speed boat
or a fat turkey
a dripping diamond necklace

it wasn't trash, though it smelled so old

he yo-yoed in his bedroom wearing his pro sleepwear
he brushed his teeth with my deluxe toothbrush
and I brushed with an ordinary one from the store

Me and Lena

Me and Lena are twins and have been the whole time.
For Halloween we used to be Siamese in a big shirt.
Lena used to choose what we wore, but then she started
to dress tight. Now we are basically adults. Whenever
I picture something romantic and naked, like when
I'm trying to get my dreams off, I picture her the one
getting done. It only makes sense, or else how am I get-
ting that view? (the side view) (or over the shoulder) So
Lena does the thing with neighborhood boys and movie
men and strangers she meets in the park. I assumed she
did the same, pictured me in her place, but no, she says
she pictures her too. I try not to let this hurt me, but it
does.

New Movement blah blah

all the grad kids called me up on the phone:
Hey come out with us, lets get funny and crazy, trade lines
and write a big fat poem!
Hmmmm, I said
I gotta go, I said, *my mom needs this line, Wait MOM, hang*
on Mom!
then hung up like there'd been a struggle

the one Lila has appointed herself big sister
and tells me about boys
like how to do things
she asks about her nose, on my walk back from school
if it looks snobby

I stroll around the library, looking very undergrad,
blending in fine
I chill out on their campus because when I'm older
that's an option
but for now my life is close and un-perverted

a week after the homeless guy hung himself at Smith
I hung from a rope around my waist
tied to the same tree
a cigarette drawn on my mouth with marker

Northampton gathered around and giggled
it wasn't political how the article said
blah blah blah

screw this early stage
I'll end up where I ought to be
in black and white photos of Art Movement Groups
from the 1920's, Paris 1880, Berlin 2020
a ferret scarf around my neck
a painter in the new movement blah blah
first on the right
behind the Donald Duck triptych
(before it was destroyed in the fire)
twice married, 3 times divorced, Lady Gruber the 1st
blinking in this photo because the flash made her so happy!
blinking in the photo because I was having an affair
with the photographer
a very insane and glamorous affair
(so glamorous that I'd run out of all my shillings, pence,
and lire)
smiling because I'd just brainstormed the forward
to the last book in my series
The awkward days of Mrs. Hayes
next to me in the photograph
(which is stained with blood and wine)
is my mentor Harold H. Smiler, an unhappy genius that

you would admire
if you ever laid eyes on him at the mouth of the Tiber
near where my soccer team meets
my new dream soccer team

Tropical Islands

a woman in the bathtub sees her nipples
and the land around them
as two tropical islands
places too exotic to visit on her salary

It is human to love houses

to see houses as an embodiment of the life one could
potentially live inside
to look at house listings for fun, while inside a house
as if life can only be lived indoors

it is natural to want an ancient house
so one might have the old, real thoughts
or a slick, new house
to have expensive, expansive thoughts

certain thoughts one could not have outside
and if one were living outside, one would create
a sort of house unconsciously
even if it were just sticks and leaves
it would be difficult to keep from arranging them
as a person is always trying to fix the area immediate to him

a room shrinks a person's universe
and in each drawer sits a smaller, more obscure universe

a person personifies their bedroom
as something that likes them
sees houses as valentines in the woods
secret novels with no sex scenes
as constant Arthur Miller plays

a human senses the dreamy brain of the structure
and converts
forgetting that houses outlive the people inside them

I wanna know which friend will die young,
so I can spend more time with them now

you hurt my feelings so I lie
and say, I do wanna fuck my roommate
I say, We've pushed our beds so they share a wall

when you were young and bumped your head on the table
your father would make a show of hitting the table

when you bumped your knee in the doorway
your father would kick the doorway
would beat the couch

I wanna know which friend will die
so I can surprise my other friends

we climb into the car
lick the cd
pick the mountain with the most views

Let's try primal scream therapy, I say
Scream as loud as you possibly can

I s c r e a m

dogs learn terrible truths

I s c r e a m

teenagers cry over the telephone

Come on, everyone try!
but no one else will
W h a t e v e r, I say
Your personality will stay the same
while my personality evolves!

I wanna know which friend it'll be
so I can tease that friend about it

we all did our part in making the bathroom disgusting
one of the cats we hated, one we revered
both we tried to lose on Craigslist

there were so many views I felt ill
on our way to the mountain, the mountain was the view
on the mountain, where'd we been was the view

I met a boy
he had a thing you could put
I had a place you could go

my boobs looked so good I had to show his kitchen

clear stuff was all over his hands
There isn't even a name for this, I said smelling his hands
That's how elusive it is

I wanna know which friend
so I can become less good friends with them

MTV had already ended
our parents were still familiar

I'm a feminist, I said to his pillow
That means I get two orgasms and you get one

I pushed the boy's balls into a shape
Stop making dick art, he said
I pushed them into another shape

Side love

most people can't help but have a side love
that runs a weak stream by their main love

it sets a subtle tone
the way religion sets a tone
it varnishes one's moments
by the fireplace

anyone who has loved is prone to love
and counts his loves on his fingers
writes their initials in a tiny box on the bottom of a page
then Xs the box

people let months go by
and then say hi to the secret love
running within them

a man gazes into his love's eyes
and is able to look out from his other love's eyes
to see a man eating his dinner

certain qualities of light
the lazy hours of captivity
the horizon allows a secret love
when the love is too flawed to walk

to indulge it is to throw down a bluffed hand

to confess it is to strangle it with complication
to proudly call a wrong number

to keep it is a kind of psychic materialism
a child's wish for more wishes

Rainbow-enthusiasts

rainbow-enthusiasts love my daughter
hers is a leaky blue light

rainbow-enthusiasts are drab dressers
they are spiritual, but not a drop religious

they wake early, sensing mist
they desire travel
they leave at once

I know
I've dated so many

they have kind, old fathers
they are good lovers

I'm talking about Trent Reznor, saying he's a Shakespearean tragic hero

one verse sounded like Edward Scissorhands
crying in the bathroom
another like rats fighting over rat bait

there was a kind of music called Industrial
or maybe there still is

all music videos took place in abandoned factories
as if that was the only place people could really let loose

there is no aesthetically pure place
even a white room is unnatural and affected
the outdoors now come with an environmental tone
a dusty landscape under the stars seems partly
European, or South American, unfortunately

Industrial music is about machines helping to make music
but then taking over the song

an Industrial song doesn't want to be loved the way
other songs would like to be loved
an Industrial song is an anti-romance
for people who don't want to enjoy things
a dark, nagging underground

Electronic music is made by new, gleaming machines
and Industrial music is made by old, dusty machines
originally built to do laundry

if something is Industrial, it makes something
humans want, but don't want to see being made
it is big, used to chemicals, cheap

Trent Reznor is his own music
I wouldn't call him Industrial
though he coaxed the anti-romance from machines
to great fortune

his music was like a black marbled composition
notebook soaking in lye
a famous person raging against their fame
a drama nerd uncovering a love affair
involving his drama teacher

music reviews are just like food reviews
though I smile when they describe the guitars
"crunching" "spangling" "heaving" "scratchy"

when I think of Industrial music
I think of a black that brightens to yellow
but I'm thinking of that Soundgarden album by mistake

of street lights lighting grime

a few years ago Trent was on his skateboard
eating a popsicle
the picture was jarring in a "universal man" way
and also an "after the music" way
more recently he married someone
and then won the Oscar, and his hair was short
and his suit was blah
he seemed very corporate, and said nothing
I thought it was lame
but now I see it's sort of Industrial of him
his body and his fate are bound, and he follows along
abandoned like a factory, alive after midnight

Dessert after dinner

the little menu is obscene
and often pushed to the center of the table

a dessert will leave the mind wildly elsewhere
slumped on a couch in Europe with the rest of them

dessert will pervert the check to an unlikely high number
an even, female number
or a meandering, troubled, male one

people who eat dessert after dinner
have sex that same evening or
observe a brief religious image
in the glass of their car

resisting dessert is dangerously moral
it can dull your senses

once the question is posed
the waiter must agree with the way your face leads you
he understands the dusty foundation of your being
he sees the junk left there by the workmen who built you

waiters and waitresses have lived hundreds of years
in a cycle of lives
on an entirely different plane

waitresses in fancy restaurants have great skin
and dark hearts
a graceful manner has been encoded inside them
they are always engaged to be married

who can say what dessert means to them?

waiters are of good height
they suspend their voice in the air
like a plank between boats

is dessert all that sustains them?
a chore that prolongs them in this body
gliding around the restaurant
wearing the required black shoes

they fall continually in and out of love
unable to find a place of despair or maintainable happiness
they select another attribute from the vast cupboard

The whale changes his mind

the computer, sick of its parts

Sally just wants someone nearby

Mother is horrid and makes us wait

and yet, the tree leans towards Gertrude

a cloud crashes over your father

teenage girls are triumphant

I am curled inside a cannon

John walks like C3P0 into the bathroom

this bee walks over our t.v.

the man is thinking of leaving his family

the minute hand keeps judging him and nudging

boiling like flowers

a classroom of dreamers

the inconsistent policeman

help yourself out of this castle

the boys are ebullient floating on their own historical disk

you wake up and wonder

any combination of things

cart the body in a daze

stop, its ruining the party

Sal is difficult at dinner

I look at Ernesto and see a change

something is pushing me to go to the movie

and at the movie, something is still pushing me

People in pain

the basic kind
a pure, invisible physicality
the rope is thin and stretches
the nerves sing through it

the pain is long
a glowing sandbar out in the nothing

the pain can be located
as a phone call to a bad apartment
a harsh inarticulate god

the pain links you with all people in pain

it is more mystical than technology
it is more natural than the northern lights
but it's related to the northern lights
babies know it
animals spend hours in the sun considering it

The bat

on the beach we found a bat and ball
I wanna swallow that ball, the ocean said flirting

the sunset was pastels was perfect and harmful
the sand was wet and would not dry

This is Georgia O'Keefe's dream, the rocks said
Georgia is dead, the sunset said back
sympathetic and gloating

the beach involved us in some baseball
one of us was the batter
stretched out in a stance
wiggling his bat high
recalling little league like a girl he'd once liked

the bat hit air
the ball rolled itself to puddles

GOD IS UP IN THAT SUNSET
HIT HIM TWEEN HIS EYES we yelled
KNOCK HIS TEETH OUT
he didn't exist and we knew it
FUCK HIS SHIT UP GOOD
but what was that sunset about

FUCK THIS GOD HIDING OUT IN THE SKY
HIT HIM IN THE BALLS we yelled

during the baseball we dug our names in the sand
the apocalypse was a daydream as it has always been
between us and between everything was a boner of love

the batter hit the ball into the water
narrowly missing the sunset

this dream of O'Keefe's wasn't the whole
vagina/flower thing
that everyone's always bringing up
this one was rocks and how they feel
when they're by themselves
the gauze the weather nets on
making everything the right colors

yelling at the sunset only made us believe in god a bit more
we weren't scared that a hand would grab us from the sunset
we wanted a hand to grab us

Special thanks to Emily Pettit, Guy Pettit, Dara Wier, Chris Cheney, Seth Landman, Mike Young, Peter Gizzi, Pam Glaven, Nat Otting, Max Bean, Mojo Lorwin, John Maradik and Jerry & Karen Glaser, all of whom helped in the creation and completion of this book.

Rachel B. Glaser is a writer, painter, and teacher living in Northampton, MA. Glaser is also the author of the story collection *Pee On Water* (Publishing Genius Press), a *'Believer'*s Readers Book of 2010.' Glaser received her B.F.A. in Painting at Rhode Island School of Design, and an M.F.A. in Fiction from the University of Massachusetts, Amherst. She teaches Creative Writing at Flying Object in Hadley, MA and has been painting basketball players for the past few years. To see more visit Rachelbglaser.blogspot.com